Henry A. Beers

The Thankless Muse

Henry A. Beers

The Thankless Muse

ISBN/EAN: 9783743303577

Manufactured in Europe, USA, Canada, Australia, Japa

Cover: Foto ©Thomas Meinert / pixelio.de

Manufactured and distributed by brebook publishing software
(www.brebook.com)

Henry A. Beers

The Thankless Muse

THE THANKLESS MUSE

BY

HENRY A. BEERS

BOSTON AND NEW YORK
HOUGHTON, MIFFLIN AND COMPANY
The Riverside Press, Cambridge
1885

PREFATORY NOTE.

THIS volume includes, with a number of new poems, a selection from a book of verses published in 1878, and entitled "Odds and Ends." Half of that edition — of five hundred copies — was consumed by the public; the other half much more rapidly by the fire which burned Messrs. Houghton, Mifflin & Co.'s Boston store in 1879.

CONTENTS.

THE THANKLESS MUSE.

THE muses ring my bell and run away.
    I spy you, rogues, behind the evergreen:
You, wanton Thalia, romper in the hay ;
    And you, Terpsichore, you long-legged quean.
When I was young you used to come and stay,
    But, now that I grow older, 't is well seen
What tricks ye put upon me.   Well-a-day !
    How many a summer evening have ye been
Sitting about my door-step, fain to sing
        And tell old tales, while through the fragrant
            dark
        Burned the large planets, throbbed the brooding
            sound
Of crickets and the tree-toads' ceaseless ring ;
        And in the meads the fire-fly lit her spark
        Where from my threshold sank the vale profound.

SPIRIT LAKE.

IT lies among the western hills
  In purple distance far away,
Fed by the gush of mountain rills
  Within the portals of the day.

Basking in summer stillness deep,
  Among the dim blue hills it gleams
Forever in a charméd sleep,
  Lulled by the flow of sounding streams.

At evening on the dusky wold
  When winds from out the sunset blow,
And in the west the waves of gold
  Suffuse the sky with liquid glow;

While in the wide extended blush
  I mark the disk of one bright star,
Tinged with a faint unearthly flush
  It shines like Heaven's gate ajar.

SPIRIT LAKE.

And when I in the midnight wake
  And through my windows see the moon,
And hear the gusty curtain shake
  And the low summer night wind's tune;

That lonely lake my spirit laves
  As in a vague and wandering dream,
And, listening to the wash of waves,
  Far on the middle mere I seem.

I see the moon-bathed waters wide;
  I hear the dip of spectral oars,
Strange echoes on the mountain side,
  Uncertain whispers on the shores.

But on thy margin, haunted pool,
  Enchantment holds her wizard throne:
Above thy spell-bound surface cool
  A mystic silence broods alone.

Across thy bosom glides no sail;
  No voice of man disturbs thy sleep;
Nor ever comes intruding gale
  To stir thy tranquil water deep.

The traveler on the lonely hill
  When dim-eyed twilight gathers round

And the brown air is moist and still,
Hears through the dusk a solemn sound,

As of the ringing of sweet bells
Within the distant mountain's breast,
And oft on rainless nights he tells
Of lightning flashes in the west.

The wild deer from the forest glade
Are gone ; but still their ghosts may slake
Their thirst, where none e'er dips the blade
In thy dark wave, O Spirit Lake.

WATER LILIES AT SUNSET.

MINE eyes have seen when once at sunset hour,
White lily flocks that edged a lonely lake
All rose and sank upon the lifting swell
That swayed their long stems lazily, and lapped
Their floating pads and stirred among the leaves.
And when the sun from western gates of day
Poured colored flames, they, kissed to ruddy shame,
So blushed through snowy petals, that they glowed
Like roses 'morning-blown in dewy bowers,
When garden-walks lie dark with early shade.
That so their perfumed chalices were brimmed
With liquid glory till they overflowed
And spilled rich lights and purple shadows out,
That splashed the pool with gold, and stained its
    waves
In tints of violet and ruby blooms.
But when the flashing gem that lit the day
Dropped in its far blue casket of the hills,
The rainbow paintings faded from the mere,
The wine-dark shades grew black, the gilding
    dimmed,

While paling slow through tender amber hues,
The crimsoned lilies blanched to coldest white,
And wanly shivered in the evening breeze.
When twilight closed — when earliest dew-drops
  fell
All frosty-chill deep down their golden hearts,
They shrank at that still touch, as maidens shrink,
When love's first footstep frights with sweet alarms
The untrod wildness of their virgin breasts;
Then shut their ivory cups, and dipping low
Their folded beauties in the gloomy wave,
They nodded drowsily and heaved in sleep.
But sweeter far than summer dreams at dawn,
Their mingled breaths from out the darkness stole,
Across the silent lake, the winding shores,
The shadowy hills that rose in lawny slopes,
The marsh among whose reeds the wild fowl
  screamed,
And dusky woodlands where the night came down.

BUMBLE BEE.

As I lay yonder in tall grass
A drunken bumble-bee went past
Delirious with honey toddy.
The golden sash about his body
Could scarce keep in his swollen belly
Distent with honey-suckle jelly.
Rose liquor and the sweet pea wine
Had filled his soul with song divine ;
Deep had he drunk the warm night through :
His hairy thighs were wet with dew.
Full many an antic he had played
While the world went round through sleep and
       shade.
Oft had he lit with thirsty lip
Some flower-cup's nectared sweets to sip,
When on smooth petals he would slip
Or over tangled stamens trip,
And headlong in the pollen rolled,
Crawl out quite dusted o'er with gold.
Or else his heavy feet would stumble

Against some bud and down he 'd tumble
Amongst the grass; there lie and grumble
In low, soft bass — poor maudlin bumble!
With tipsy hum on sleepy wing
He buzzed a glee — a bacchic thing
Which, wandering strangely in the moon,
He learned from grigs that sing in June,
Unknown to sober bees who dwell
Through the dark hours in waxen cell.
When south wind floated him away
The music of the summer day
Lost something: sure it was a pain
To miss that dainty star-light strain.

THE OLD CITY.

ANCIENT city, down thy street
Minstrels make their music sweet;
Sound of bells is on the air,
Fountains sing in every square,
Where, from dawn to shut of day,
Maidens walk and children play;
And at night, when all are gone,
The waters in the dark sing on,
Till the moonrise and the breeze
Whiten the horse-chestnut trees.
Cool thou liest, leisured, slow,
On the plains of long ago,
All unvexed of fretful trades
Through thy rich and dim arcades,
Overlooking lands below
Terraced to thy green plateau.

Dear old city, it is long
Since I heard thy minstrels' song,
Since I heard thy church-bells deep,
Since I watched thy fountains leap.

Yet, whichever way I turn,
Still I see the sunset burn
At the ending of the street,
Where the chestnut branches meet ;
Where, between the gay bazaars,
Maidens walk with eyes like stars,
And the slippered merchants go
On the pavements to and fro.
Upland winds blow through my sleep,
Moonrise glimmers, waters leap,
Till, awaking, thou dost seem
Like a city of a dream, —
Like a city of the air,
Builded high, aloof and fair, —
Such as childhood used to know
On the plains of long ago.

AS YOU LIKE IT.

HERE while I read the light forsakes the pane;
    Metempsychosis of the twilight gray —
Into green aisles of Epping or Ardenne
    The level lines of print stretch far away.

The book-leaves whisper like the forest-leaves;
    A smell of ancient woods, a breeze of morn,
A breath of violets from the mossy paths,
    And hark ! the voice of hounds — the royal horn,

Which, muffled in the ferny coverts deep,
    Utters the three sweet notes that sound recall;
As, riding two by two between the oaks,
    Come on the paladins and ladies all.

The court will rest from chase in this smooth glade
    That slopes to meet yon little rushy stream,
Where in the shallows nod the arrow-heads,
    And the blue flower-de-luce's banners gleam.

The gamekeepers are coupling of the hounds;
  The pages hang bright scarfs upon the boughs;
The new-slain quarry lies upon the turf
  Whereon but now he with the herd did browse.

The silk pavilion shines among the trees;
  The mighty pasties and the flagons strong
Give cheer to the dear heart of many a knight,
  And many a dame whose beauty lives in song.

Meanwhile a staging improvised and rude
  Rises, whereon the masquers and the mines
Play for their sport a pleasant interlude,
  Fantastic, gallant, pointing at the times.

Their green-room is the wide midsummer wood;
  Down some far-winding gallery the deer —
The dappled dead-head of that sylvan show —
  Starts as the distant ranting strikes his ear.

They use no traverses nor painted screen
  To help along their naked, out-door wit:
(Only the forest lends its leafy scene)
  Yet wonderfully well they please the pit.

The plaudits echo through the wide parquet
  Where the fair audience upon the grass,

Each knight beside his lady-love, is set,
  While overhead the merry winds do pass.

The little river murmurs in its reeds,
  And somewhere in the verdurous solitude
The wood-thrush drops a cool contralto note,
  An orchestra well-tuned unto their mood.

As runs the play so runs the afternoon ;
  The curtain and the sun fall side by side ;
The epilogue is spoke, the twilight come ;
  Then homeward through the darkening glades
    they ride.

BETWEEN THE FLOWERS.

An open door and door-steps wide,
With pillared vines on either side,
And terraced flowers, stair over stair,
Standing in pots of earthenware
Where stiff processions filed around —
Black on the smooth, sienna ground.
Tubers and bulbs now blossomed there
Which, in the moisty hot-house air,
Lay winter long in patient rows,
Glassed snugly in from Christmas snows :
Tuberoses, with white, waxy gems
In bunches on their reed-like stems;
Their fragrance forced by art too soon
To mingle with the sweets of June.
(So breathes the thin blue smoke, that steals
From ashes of the gilt pastilles,
Burnt slowly, as the brazier swings,
In dim saloons of eastern kings.)
I saw the calla's arching cup
With yellow spadix standing up,

Its liquid scents to stir and mix —
The goldenest of toddy-sticks ;
Roses and purple fuchsia drops ;
Camellias, which the gardener crops
To make the sickening wreaths that lie
On coffins when our loved ones die.
These all and many more were there ;
Monsters and *grandifloras* rare,
With tropical broad leaves, grown rank
Drinking the waters of the tank
Wherein the lotus-lilies bathe ;
All curious forms of spur and spathe,
Pitcher and sac and cactus-thorn,
There in the fresh New England morn.
But where the sun came colored through
Translucent petals wet with dew,
The interspace was carpeted
With oriel lights and nodes of red,
Orange and blue and violet,
That wove strange figures, as they met,
Of airier tissue, brighter blooms
Than tumble from the Persian looms.
So at the pontiffs' feasts, they tell,
From the board's edge the goblet fell,
Spilled from its throat the purple tide
And stained the pavement far and wide.

Such steps wise Sheba trod upon
Up to the throne of Solomon ;
So bright the angel-crowded steep
Which Israel's vision scaled in sleep.
What one is she whose feet shall dare
Tread that illuminated stair ?
Like Sheba, queen ; like angels, fair ?
Oh listen ! In the morning air
The blossoms all are hanging still —
The queen is standing on the sill.
No Sheba she ; her virgin zone
Proclaims her royalty alone :
(Such royalty the lions own.)
Yet all too cheap the patterned stone
That paves kings' palaces, to feel
The pressure of her gaiter's heel.
The girlish grace that lit her face
Made sunshine in a dusky place —
The old silk hood, demure and quaint,
Wherein she seemed an altar-saint
Fresh-tinted, though in setting old
Of dingy carving and tarnished gold ;
Her eyes, the candles in that shrine,
Making Madonna's face to shine.
Lingering I passed, but evermore
Abide with me the open door,

The doorsteps wide, the flowers that stand
In brilliant ranks on either hand,
The two white pillars and the vine
Of bitter-sweet and lush woodbine,
And — from my weary paths as far
As Sheba or the angels are —
Between, upon the wooden sill,
Thou, Queen of Hearts, art standing still.

BEAVER POND MEADOW.

Thou art my Dismal Swamp, my Everglades:
Thou my Campagna, where the bison wades
Through shallow, steaming pools, and the sick air
Decays. Thou my Serbonian Bog art, where
O'er leagues of mud, black vomit of the Nile,
Crawls in the sun the myriad crocodile.
Or thou my Cambridge or my Lincoln fen
Shalt be — a lonely land where stilted men
Stalking across the surface waters go,
Casting long shadows, and the creaking, slow
Canal-barge, laden with its marshy hay,
Disturbs the stagnant ditches twice a day.
Thou hast *thy* crocodiles: on rotten logs
Afloat, the turtles swarm and bask: the frogs,
When come the pale, cold twilights of the spring,
Like distant sleigh-bells through the meadows ring.
The school-boy comes on holidays to take
The musk-rat in its hole, or kill the snake,
Or fish for bull-heads in the pond at night.
The hog-snout's swollen corpse, with belly white,
I find upon the footway through the sedge,

Trodden by tramps along the water's edge.
Not thine the breath of the salt marsh below
Where, when the tide is out, the mowers go
Shearing the oozy plain, that reeks with brine
More tonic than the incense of the pine.
Thou art the sink of all uncleanliness,
A drain for slaughter-pens, a wilderness
Of trenches, pockets, quagmires, bogs where rank
The poison sumach grows, and in the tank
The water standeth ever black and deep
Greened o'er with scum : foul pottages, that steep
And brew in that dark broth, at night distil
Malarious fogs bringing the fever chill.
Yet grislier horrors thy recesses hold :
The murdered peddler's body five days old
Among the yellow lily-pads was found
In yonder pond : the new-born babe lay drowned
And throttled on the bottom of this moat,
Near where the negro hermit keeps his boat ;
Whose wigwam stands beside the swamp ; whose
    meals
It furnishes, fat pouts and mud-spawned eels.
Even so thou hast a kind of beauty, wild,
Unwholesome — thou the suburb's outcast child,
Behind whose grimy skin and matted hair
Warm nature works and makes her creature fair.
  8

Summer has wrought a blue and silver border
Of iris flags and flowers in triple order
Of the white arrowhead round Beaver Pond,
And o'er the milkweeds in the swamp beyond
Tangled the dodder's amber-colored threads.
In every fosse the bladderwort's bright heads
Like orange helmets on the surface show.
Richer surprises still thou hast : I know
The ways that to thy penetralia lead,
Where in black bogs the sundew's sticky bead
Ensnares young insects, and that rosy lass,
Sweet Arethusa, blushes in the grass.
Once on a Sunday when the bells were still,
Following the path under the sandy hill
Through the old orchard and across the plank
That bridges the dead stream, past many a rank
Of cat-tails, midway in the swamp I found
A small green mead of dry but spongy ground,
Entrenched about on every side with sluices
Full to the brim of thick lethean juices,
The filterings of the marsh.   With line and hook
Two little French boys from the trenches took
Frogs for their Sunday meal and gathered messes
Of pungent salad from the water-cresses.
A little isle of foreign soil it seemed,
And listening to their outland talk, I dreamed

That yonder spire above the elm-tops calm
Rose from the village chestnuts of La Balme.
Yes, many a pretty secret hast thou shown
To me, O Beaver Pond, walking alone
On summer afternoons, while yet the swallow
Skimmed o'er each flaggy plash and gravelly shal-
      low ;
Or when September turned the swamps to gold
And purple.   But the year is growing old :
The golden-rod is rusted, and the red
That streaked October's frosty cheek is dead ;
Only the sumach's garnet pompons make
Procession through the melancholy brake.
Lo! even now the autumnal wind blows cool
Over the rippled waters of thy pool,
And red autumnal sunset colors brood
Where I alone and all too late intrude.

NARCISSUS.

WHERE the black hemlock slants athwart the stream
He came to bathe ; the sun's pursuing beam
Laid a warm hand upon him, as he stood
Naked, while noonday silence filled the wood.
Holding the boughs o'erhead, with cautious foot
He felt his way along the mossy root
That edged the brimming pool; then paused and
      dreamed.
Half like a dryad of the tree he seemed,
Half like the naiad of the stream below,
Suspended there between the water's flow
And the green tree-top world ; the love-sick air
Coaxing with softest touch his body fair
A little longer yet to be content
Outside of its own crystal element.
And he, still lingering at the brink, looked down
And marked the sunshine fleck with gold the
      brown
And sandy floor which paved that woodland pool.
But then, within the shadows deep and cool

Which the close hemlocks on the surface made,
Two eyes met his yet darker than that shade
And, shining through the watery foliage dim,
Two white and slender arms reached up to him.
"Comest thou again, now all the woods are still,
Fair shape, nor even Echo from the hill
Calls her Narcissus? Would her voice were thine,
Dear speechless image, and could answer mine!
Her I but hear and thee I may but see;
Yet, Echo, thou art happy unto me;
For though thyself art but a voice, sad maid,
Thy love the substance is and my love shade.
Alas! for never may I kiss those dumb
Sweet lips, nor ever hope to come
Into that shadow-world that lies somewhere —
Somewhere between the water and the air.
Alas! for never shall I clasp that form
That mocks me yonder, seeming firm and warm;
But if I leap to its embrace, the cold
And yielding flood is all my arms enfold.
All creatures else, save only me, can share
My beauties, be it but to stroke my hair,
Or hold my hand in theirs, or hear me speak.
The village wives will laugh and clap my cheek;
The forest nymphs will beg me for a kiss,
To make me blush, or hide themselves by this

Clear brook to see me bathe. But I must pine,
Loving not me but this dear ghost of mine."
Then, bending down the boughs, until they dipped
Their broad green fronds, into the wave he slipped,
And, floating breast-high, from the branches hung,
His body with the current idly swung.
And ever and anon he caught the gleam
Of a white shoulder swimming in the stream,
Pressed close to his, and two young eyes of black
Under the dimpling surface answered back
His own, just out of kissing distance: then
The vain and passionate longing came again
Still baffled, still renewed: he loosed his hold
Upon the boughs and strove once more to fold
To his embrace that fine unbodied shape;
But the quick apparition made escape,
And once again his empty arms took in
Only the water and the shadows thin.
Thus every day, when noon lay bright and hot
On all the plains, there came to this cool spot,
Under the hemlocks by the deepening brook,
Narcissus, Phœbus' darling, there to look
And pore upon his picture in the flood:
Till once a peeping dryad of the wood,
Tracking his steps along the slender path
Which he between the tree trunks trodden hath,

Misses the boy on whom her amorous eyes
Were wont to feed; but where he stood she spies
A new-made yellow flower, that still doth seem
To woo his own pale reflex in the stream;
Whom Phœbus kisses when the woods are still
And only ceaseless Echo from the hill
Unprompted cries *Narcissus!*

ON A MINIATURE.

THINE old-world eyes — each one a violet
    Big as the baby rose that is thy mouth —
Set me a dreaming.   Have our eyes not met
    In childhood — in a garden of the South?

Thy lips are trembling with a song of France,
    My cousin, and thine eyes are dimly sweet;
'Wildered with reading in an old romance
    All afternoon upon the garden seat.

The summer wind read with thee, and the bees
    That on the sunny pages loved to crawl:
A skipping reader was the impatient breeze,
    And turned the leaves, but the slow bees read
        all.

And now thy foot descends the terrace stair:
    I hear the rustle of thy silk attire;
I breathe the musky odors of thy hair
    And airs that from thy painted fan respire.

Idly thou pausest in the shady walk,
  Thine ear attentive to the fountain's fall:
Thou mark'st the flower-de-luce sway on her stalk,
  The speckled vergalieus ripening on the wall.

Thou hast the feature of my mother's race,
  The gilded comb she wore, her smile, her eye :
The blood that flushes softly in thy face
  Crawls through my veins beneath this northern
    sky.

As one disherited, though next of kin,
  Who lingers at the barred ancestral gate,
And sadly sees the happy heir within
  Stroll careless through his forfeited estate ;

Even so I watch thy southern eyes, Lisette,
  Lady of my lost paradise and heir
Of summer days that were my birthright. Yet
  Beauty like thine makes usurpation fair.

KATY DID.

In a windy tree-top sitting,
  Singing at the fall of dew,
Katy watched the bats a-flitting,
  While the twilight's curtains drew
Closer round her; till she only
  Saw the branches and the sky —
Rocking late and rocking lonely,
  Anchored on the darkness high.
And the song that she was singing,
In the windy tree-tops swinging,   ·
Was *under the tree, under the tree*
The fox is digging a pit for me.

When the early stars were sparkling
  Overhead, and down below
Fireflies twinkled, through the darkling
  Thickets she heard footsteps go —
Voice of her false lover speaking,
  Laughing to his sweetheart new : —
"Half my heart for thee I'm breaking :
  Did not Katy love me true?"

Then no longer she was singing,
But through all the wood kept ringing —
Katy did, Katy did, Katy did love thee
And the fox is digging a grave for me.

IM SCHWARZWALD.

THE winter sunset, red upon the snow,
Lights up the narrow way that I should go;
Winding o'er bare white hilltops, whereon lie
Dark churches and the holy evening sky.
That path would lead me deep into the west,
Even to the feet of her I love the best.

But this scarce broken track in which I stand
Runs east, up through the tan-woods' midnight
   land;
Where now the newly risen moon doth throw
The shadows of long stems across the snow.
This path would take me to the Jäger's Tree
Where stands the Swabian girl and waits for me.

Her eyes are blacker than the woods at night
And witching as the moon's uncertain light;
And there are tones in that low voice of hers
Caught from the wind among the Schwarzwald firs,
And from the Gutach's echoing waters, when
Still evening listens in the Forsthaus glen.

I must — I must! Thou wilt forgive me, sweet;
My heart flies west but eastward move my feet;
The mad moon brightens as the sunset dies,
And yonder hexie draws me with her eyes.
Ruck, ruck an meine grüne Seit' she sings
And with her arms the frozen trunk enrings,

And lays upon its bark her little face.
How canst thou be so dead in her embrace —
So cold against her kisses, happy tree?
Thou hast no love beyond the western sea.
Methinks that at the lightest touch of her
Thy wooden trunk should tremble, thy boughs
    stir :

But at the pressure of her tender form
Thy inmost pith should feel her and grow warm:
The torpid sap should race along the vein;
The resinous buds should swell, and once again
Fresh needles shoot, as though the breeze of
    spring
Already through the woods came whispering.

VITTORIA COLONNA.

A POET's daughter and a poet's bride,
  A poet's self thou art, — nay, more, far more :
The moon thou art, that flings a heart's wild tide
  In wordless music on fate's iron shore.

Children he hath begot of thee, and songs :
  My love is barren as the desert sea.
Salt weed it bears, and for a tongue it longs,
  But in its deeps are gold and pearl for thee.

He hath his will of thee : in life, in death,
  I shall thy beggar be, and he thy king ;
Yet, though a thousand trifles claim my breath,
  Of my one love for thee I may not sing.

Leave off thy loving ! Is there nothing mine?
  Rise up, fresh kissed, from off thy husband's
      knee ;
Fling wide the blind, and let thy hearth-fire shine
  One moment on the jealous, homeless sea.

WON.

At last I have thee safe;
Thou wilt no longer chafe
    Against the chain.   ·
Thou canst not, though thou would,
Be aught but true and good
    Ever again.

Yes, now thou art my wife;
The suit to win, the strife
    To keep, are o'er.
The weakness of the flesh,
The spirit's waywardness,
    Will vex no more.

No more will anger harm
Nor jealousy alarm,
    Now thou art mine.
Thy other lovers all,
Hearing that grim recall,
    The chase resign.

They do not greatly care
If thou be foul or fair,
   Single or wed.
To me they yield their claim
On body, soul, and name, —
   Now thou art dead.

WAITING FOR WINTER.

WHAT honey in the year's last flowers can hide,
  These little yellow butterflies may know :
  With falling leaves they waver to and fro,
Or on the swinging tops of asters ride.
But I am weary of the summer's pride
  And sick September's simulated show :
  Why do the colder winds delay to blow
And bring the pleasant hours that we abide ;
To curtained alcove and sweet household talks,
  Or sweeter silence by our flickering Lars,
Returning late from autumn evening walks
  Upon the frosty hills, while reddening Mars
Hangs low between the withered mullein stalks,
  And upward throngs the host of winter stars ?

Tò Πᾶν.

THE little creek which yesterday I saw
　　Ooze through the sedges, and each brackish
　　　　vein
　　That sluiced the marsh, now filled and then
　　　　again
Sucked dry to glut the sea's unsated maw,
All ebb and flow by the same rhythmic law
　　That times the beat of the Atlantic main —
　　They also fastened to the swift moon's train
By unseen cords that no less strongly draw.
So, poet, may thy life's small tributary
　　Threading some bitter marsh, obscure, alone,
Feel yet one pulse with the broad estuary
　　That bears an emperor's fleets through half a
　　　　zone:
May wait upon the same high luminary
　　And pitch its voice to the same ocean's tone.

THE SINGER OF ONE SONG.

HE sang one song and died — no more but that :
  A single song and carelessly complete.
  He would not bind and thresh his chance-grown
    wheat,
Nor bring his wild fruit to the common vat,
To store the acid rinsings, thin and flat,
  Squeezed from the press or trodden under feet.
  A few slow beads, blood-red and honey-sweet,
Oozed from the grape, which burst and spilled its
    fat.
But Time, who soonest drops the heaviest things
  That weight his pack, will carry diamonds long.
    So through the poets' orchestra, which weaves
One music from a thousand stops and strings,
  Pierces the note of that immortal song : —
    " High over all the lonely bugle grieves."

AMETHYSTS.

Not the green eaves of our young woods alone
  Shelter new violets, by the spring rains kissed;
In the hard quartz, by some old April sown,
  Blossoms Time's flower, the steadfast amethyst.

"Here's pansies, they're for thoughts" — weak
      thoughts though fair; ·
June sees their opening, June their swift decay.
But those stone bourgeons stand for thoughts
      more rare,
  Whose patient crystals colored day by day.

Might I so cut my flowers within the rock,
  And prison there their sweet escaping breath;
Their petals then the winter's frost should mock,
  And only Time's slow chisel work their death.

If out of those embedded purple blooms
  Were quarried cups to hold the purple wine,
Greek drinkers thought the glorious, maddening
      fumes
  · Were cooled with radiance of that gem divine.

Might I so wed the crystal and the grape,
  Passion's red heart and plastic Art's endeavor,
Delirium should take on immortal shape,
  Dancing and blushing in strong rock forever.

POSTHUMOUS.

PUT them in print?
Make one more dint
In the ages' furrowed rock? No, no !
Let his name and his verses go.
These idle scraps, they would but wrong
His memory, whom we honored long;
And men would ask: "Is this the best —
Is this the whole his life expressed ?"
Haply he had no care to tell
To all the thoughts which flung their spell
Around us when the night grew deep,
Making it seem a loss to sleep,
Exalting the low, dingy room
To some high auditorium.
And when we parted homeward, still
They followed us beyond the hill.
The heaven had brought new stars to sight,
Opening the map of later night ;
And the wide silence of the snow,
  And the dark whispers of the pines,

And those keen fires that glittered slow
  Along the zodiac's wintry signs,
Seemed witnesses and near of kin
To the high dreams we held within.

Yet what is left
To us bereft,
Save these remains,
Which now the moth
Will fret, or swifter fire consume?
These inky stains
On his table-cloth;
These prints that decked his room;
His throne, this ragged easy-chair;
This battered pipe, his councillor.
This is the sum and inventory.
No son he left to tell his story,
No gold, no lands, no fame, no book.
Yet one of us, his heirs, who took
The impress of his brain and heart,
May gain from Heaven the lucky art
His untold meanings to impart
In words that will not soon decay.
Then gratefully will such one say:
"This phrase, dear friend, perhaps, is mine;
The breath that gave it life was thine."

CARÇAMON.

His steed was old, his armor worn,
   And he was old and worn and gray:
The light that lit his patient eyes
   It shone from very far away.

Through gay Provence he journeyed on;
   To one high quest his life was true,
And so they called him *Carçamon* —
   The knight who seeketh the world through.

A pansy blossomed on his shield;
   "A token 'tis," the people say,
"That still across the world's wide field
   He seeks *la dame de ses pensées*."

For somewhere on a painted wall,
   Or in the city's shifting crowd,
Or looking from a casement tall,
   Or shaped of dream or evening cloud —

Forgotten when, forgotten where —
  Her face had filled his careless eye
A moment ere he turned and passed,
  Nor knew it was his destiny.

But ever in his dreams it came
  Divine and passionless and strong,
A smile upon the imperial lips
  No lover's kiss had dared to wrong.

He took his armor from the wall —
  Ah! gone since then was many a day —
He led his steed from out the stall
  And sought *la dame de ses pensées.*

The ladies of the Troubadours
  Came riding through the chestnut grove
" Sir Minstrel, string that lute of yours
  And sing us a gay song of love."

"O ladies of the Troubadours,
  My lute has but a single string;
Sirventes fit for paramours,
  My heart is not in tune to sing.

"The flower that blooms upon my shield
  It has another soil and spring

Than that wherein the gaudy rose
  Of light Provence is blossoming.

"The lady of my dreams doth hold
  Such royal state within my mind,
No thought that comes unclad in gold
  To that high court may entrance find."

So through the chestnut groves he passed,
  And through the land and far away;
Nor know I whether in the world
  He found *la dame de ses pensées.*

Only I know that in the South
  Long to the harp his tale was told;
Sweet as new wine within the mouth
  The small, choice words and music old.

To scorn the promise of the real;
  To seek and seek and not to find;
Yet cherish still the fair ideal —
  It is thy fate, O restless Mind!

PSYCHE.

AT evening in the port she lay,
　　A lifeless block with canvas furled;
But silently at peep of day
˙Spread her white wings and skimmed away
And, rosy in the dawn's first ray,
　　Sunk down behind the rounding world.

So hast thou vanished from our side,
　　Dear bark, that from some far, bright strand
Anchored a while on life's dull tide;
Then, lifting spirit pinions wide,
In Heaven's own orient glorified,
　　Steered outward seeking Holy Land.

SURSUM CORDA!

TAKE courage, heart. Why dost thou faint and
    falter?
Why is thy light turned darkness ere the noon?
The wind blows west, no clouds the heaven alter,
    Night comes not yet; with night, too, comes the
    moon.

"Alas, alas! the dewy morning weather,
    The tender light that on the meadows lay,
When Youth and Hope and I set out together, —
    Light Youth, false Hope, that left me on the
    way!"

Take courage yet; thou art not unattended :
    See Love and Peace keep step on either hand.
How green the vales! The sky how blue! How
    splendid
    The strong white sunshine sleeps across the
    land!

" Alas . tne thrushes' song hath long had ending
   I heard at dawn among the pine woods cool.
The brook is still, whose rocky stair descending,
   I drank at sunrise from each rosy pool."

The noon is still ; the songs of dawn are over ;
   Yet turn not back to prove thy memories vain.
The mist upon the hills canst thou recover,
   Or bring to eastern skies the bloom again ?

But courage still !   Without return or swerving,
   Across the globe's huge shadow keep the track,
Till, unperceived, the slow meridian's curving,
   That leads thee onward, yet shall lead thee back,

To stand again with daybreak on the mountains,
   And, where the paths of night and morning meet,
To drink once more of youth's forgotten fountains,
   When thou hast put the world between thy feet.

THE RISING OF THE CURTAIN.

We sit before the curtain, and we heed the pleasant
  bustle :
The ushers hastening up the aisles, the fans' and
  programmes' rustle ;
The boy that cries librettos, and the soft, incessant
  sound
Of talking and low laughter that buzzes all around.

How very old the drop-scene looks ! A thousand
  times before
I 've seen that blue paint dashing on that red dis-
  temper shore ;
The castle and the *guazzo* sky, the very ilex-tree, —
They have been there a thousand years, — a thousand more shall be.

All our lives we have been waiting for that weary
  daub to rise ;
We have peeped behind its edges, "as if we were
  God's spies ;"

We have listened for the signal ; yet still, as in our
    youth,
The colored screen of matter hangs between us and
    the truth.

When in my careless childhood I dwelt beside a
    wood,
I tired of the clearing where my father's cabin
    stood ;
And of the wild young forest paths that coaxed me
    to explore,
Then dwindled down, or led me back to where I
    stood before.

But through the woods before our door a wagon
    track went by,
Above whose utmost western edge there hung an
    open sky ;
And there it seemed to make a plunge, or break off
    suddenly,
As though beneath that open sky it met the open
    sea.

Oh, often have I fancied, in the sunset's dreamy
    glow,
That mine eyes had caught the welter of the ocean
    waves below ;

And the wind among the pine-tops, with its low
    and ceaseless roar,
Was but an echo from the surf on that imagined
    shore.

Alas ! as I grew older, I found that road led down
To no more fair horizon than the squalid factory
    town :
So all life's purple distances, when nearer them I
    came,
Have played me still the same old cheat, — the
    same, the same, the same !

And when, O King, the heaven departeth as a
    scroll,
Wilt thou once more the promise break thou madest
    to my soul ?
Shall I see thy feasting presence thronged with
    baron, knight, and page ?
Or will the curtain rise upon a dark and empty
    stage ?

For lo, quick undulations across the canvas run ;
The foot-lights brighten suddenly, the orchestra has
    done ;

And through the expectant silence rings loud the
    prompter's bell ;
The curtain shakes, — it rises. Farewell, dull
    world, farewell !

THE IDEAS OF THE PURE REASON.

I saw in dreams a constellation strange,
Thwarting the night; its big stars seemed to range
Northward across the zenith, and to keep
Calm footing along heaven's ridge-pole high,
While round the pole the sullen Bear did creep
And dizzily the wheeling spheres went by.
They from their watch-towers in the topmost sky
Looked down upon the rest,
Nor eastward swerved nor west,
Though Procyon's candle dipped below the verge,
And the great twins of Leda 'gan decline
Toward the horizon line,
And prone Orion, sprawling headlong, urge
His flight into the far Pacific surge.

I heard a voice which said: "Those wonders
        bright
Are hung not on the hinges of the night;
But set to vaster harmonies, they run
Straight on, and turn not with the turning sphere,
Nor make an orbit about any sun.

No glass can track the courses that they steer,
By what dark paths they vanish and appear.
The starry flocks that still
Are climbing heaven's hill
Will pasture westward down its sloping lawn ;
But yon wild herd of planets, — who can say
Through what far fields they stray,
Around what focus their ellipse is drawn,
Whose shining makes their transcendental dawn ? "

I told my vision to a learned man,
Who said : " On no celestial globe or plan
Can those unset, unrisen stars be found.
How might such uncomputed motions be
Among the ordered spheres ? Heaven's clock is
     wound
To keep one time. Idle our dreams, and we,
Blown by the wind, as the light family
Of leaves." But still I dream,
And still those planets seem
Through heaven their high, unbending course to
     take ;
And a voice cries : " Freedom and Truth are we,
And Immortality :
God is our sun." And though the morning break
Across my soul still plays their shimmering wake.

TO IMOGEN AT THE HARP.

Die Geisterwelt ist nicht verschlossen:
Dein Sinn ist zu — dein Herz ist todt.
Auf, bade, Schüler, unverdrossen
Die ird'sche Brust im Morgenroth !

FAUST.

HAST thou seen ghosts ? Hast thou at midnight
    heard
In the wind's talking an articulate word?
Or art thou in the secret of the sea,
And have the twilight woods confessed to thee ?
So wild thy song, thy smile so faint, so far
Thine absent eyes from earthly vision are.
Thy song is done : why art thou listening ?
Spent is the last vibration of the string
Along the waves of sound.   Oh, doth thine ear
Pursue the ebbing chord in some fine sphere,
Where wraiths of vanished echoes live and roam,
And where thy thoughts, here strangered, find a
    home ?
Teach me the path to that uncharted land ;
Discovery's keel hath never notched its strand,

No passport may unbar its sealed frontier, —
Too far for utmost sight, for touch too near.
Subtler than light, yet all opaque, the screen
Which shuts us from that world, outspread between
The shows of sense ; like as an ether thin
Fills the vast microscopic space wherein
The molecules of matter lie enisled.
A world whose sound our silence is ; too wild
Its elfin music beats, too shrill, too rare,
To stir the slow pulse of our thicker air.
A world whose light our darkness is ; that lies
With its sharp edges turned toward mortal eyes,
Like figures painted on a folded fan —
The broken colors of some hidden plan.
The few who but an instant's look have had
At the spread pattern broadwise have gone mad.
As in a high-walled oriental street
A sudden door flies open, and a fleet
Departing dream the thirsty traveler sees
Of fountains leaping in the shade of trees,
So they who once have caught the glimpse divine :
They have but wet their lips with goblins' wine,
And, plagued with thirst immortal, must endure
The visions of the heavenly calenture, —
Of springs and dewy evening meadows rave,
While hotly round them shines the tropic wave,

And the false islands of mirage appear,
Uplifted from some transcendental sphere
Far down below the blue horizon line.
And thirst like theirs is nursed by songs like thine.
For thou, in some crepuscular dim hour,
When the weak umber moon had hardly power
To cast a shadow, and a wind, half-spent,
Creeping among the way-side bushes went,
Hast seen a cobweb spun across the moon,
A faint eclipse, penumbral, gone full soon,
Yet marking on the planet's smoky ring
A silhouette as of a living thing.
Or on the beach making thy lonely range,
Close upon sunset, when the light was strange
And the low wind had meanings, thou hast known
A presence nigh, betrayed by shadows thrown
On the red sand from bodies out of sight ;
Even as, by the shell of curving light
Pared from the dark moon's edge, the eye can tell
Where her full circle rounds invisible.

Teach me the path into that silent land.
Take once again the haunted wires in hand,
And pour the strain which, waking, thou hast heard
Whistled when night was deep by some lone bird
Hid in the dark and dewy sycamore, —   ·

When thou hast risen and unbarred the door
And walked the garden paths till night was flown,
Listening the message sent to thee alone.
Ah ! once again thy harp, thy voice once more,
Fling back the refluent tide upon the shore.
All nature grows unearthly ; all things seem
To break and waver off in shapes of dream,
And through the chinks of matter steals the dawn
Of skies beyond the solar road withdrawn.
Oh, flood my soul with that pure morning-red !
It is the sense that 's shut, the heart that 's dead :
All open still the world of spirits lies
Would we but bathe us in its red sunrise.

ECCE IN DESERTO.

THE wilderness a secret keeps
   Upon whose guess I go :
Eye hath not seen, ear hath not heard ;
   And yet I know, I know,

Some day the viewless latch will lift,
   The door of air swing wide
To one lost chamber of the wood
   Where those shy mysteries hide, —

One yet unfound, receding depth,
   From which the wood-thrush sings,
Still luring in to darker shades,
   In — in to colder springs.

There is no wind abroad to-day.
   But hark ! — the pine-tops' roar,
That sleep and in their dreams repeat
   The music of the shore.

What wisdom in their needles stirs?
  What song is that they sing?
Those airs that search the forest's heart,
  What rumor do they bring?

A hushed excitement fills the gloom,
  And, in the stillness, clear
The vireo's tell-tale warning rings :
  "' T is near — 't is near — 't is near ! "

As, in the fairy-tale, more loud
  The ghostly music plays
When, toward the enchanted bower, the prince
  Draws closer through the maze.

Nay — nay. I track a fleeter game,
  A wilder than ye know,
To lairs beyond the inmost haunt
  Of thrush or vireo.

This way it passed : the scent lies fresh ;
  The ferns still lightly shake.
Ever I follow hard upon,
  But never overtake.

  5

ECCE IN DESERTO.

To other woods the trail leads on,
  To other worlds and new,
Where they who keep the secret here
  Will keep the promise too.

HUGH LATIMER.

His lips amid the flame outsent
  A music strong and sweet,
Like some unearthly instrument
  That 's played upon by heat.

As spice-wood tough, laid on the coal,
  Sets all its perfume free,
The incense of his hardy soul
  Rose up exceedingly.

To open that great flower, too cold
  Were sun and vernal rain ;
But fire has forced it to unfold,
  Nor will it shut again.

JEANNE D'ARC.

Past midnight long! The moon hath set;
  I heard the cock an hour ago.
Still dark! no glimpse of dawn as yet,
  Though morning winds begin to blow.
Dear Lord, how swift the time goes by!
There's something in the air that rings —
Listen! — a whirring as of wings —
The myriad moments as they fly.
O fold me in thine arms, sweet night;
  Sweet pitying darkness, longer stay,
And veil me from the cruel light
  That creeps to steal my life away.

Lo! even now the waning stars
  Grow pale. The matin bell doth toll:
Prisoned like me by casement bars,
  It wakes sad echoes in my soul.
For memories woven in the braid
Of sound, bring back the abbey bell
That wont to ring when twilight fell,
  Through pastures where my childhood strayed,

What time, when flocks were in the fold,
Saint Agnes and Saint Catharine
    Looked from the darkening heavens cold,
    And wondrous Voices spake with mine.

Slow-winding Meuse, I would that still,
    Along thy grassy valleys deep,
Or half-way up some neighboring hill,
    I heard the bleat of simple sheep.
It might not be: Cassandra-wise
    I caught in dreams the din of shields;
    Far trumpets blown on tented fields
Summoned to deeds of high emprise.
    Sweet household cheer was not for me;
The pleasant hum of spinning-wheel,
    And children's prattle at my knee —
The bliss that lowly mothers feel.

My spirit winged to bolder flights,
    Drawn skyward in ecstatic dreams —
An eagle on the lonely heights,
    No ringdove haunting woodland streams.
O solemn joy! O blessed trance,
    That seized me when the drums did roll,
    And chanting priests in hood and stole
Led on the bannered hosts of France!

In battle winds above me blown
— Fit sign for maiden chevalier —
White lilies streamed, and round me shone
Strange lights, and Voices filled my ear

Foretelling victory, saying " Ride !
Ride onward, mailed in conquering might.
God's legions muster on thy side
    To stead thee in the coming fight."
When swords were sheathed and bows unstrung,
    What visions awed me as I kneeled,
    While down long aisles Te Deums pealed,
And such triumphant anthems rung,
    As Miriam, on the Red Sea shore,
Exulting to the timbrel's sound,
    Sung, when amid the loud waves' roar
Chariot and horse and rider drowned !

Ay me ! 'Tis past ; the battle 's won ;
    The Warrior breaks His useless brand.
Yet even so : His will be done
    Who holdeth victory in His hand.
I know that ere the sun is high,
    On housetop, wall, and balcony,
    Children will clap their hands with glee,
To see the Witch of Orleans die ;

And women flout me in the face
Who erst have crossed them at my name,
When in the gazing market-place
My flesh shall feed the hungry flame.

'Twere fit that guns should boom my knell,
Flags droop and funeral music roll ;
And through high minster vaults should swell
Sad requiems for my parted soul.
Crowned kings should kneel beside me dead :
Cathedral saints on storied panes,
Where daylight turns to ruby stains,
Should shed their halos round my head.
From nooks in arches twilight-dim,
And niches in the pictured wall,
Stone Christs and carven cherubim
Should look upon my broidered pall.

Alas ! for me nor passing bell,
Nor priest to shrive, nor nun to pray.
But rising smoke my death shall tell,
And whistling flames my masses say.
And if among the jeering crowd
Some lonely, beggared knight-at-arms
There be, who once in war's alarms
Hath seen me when the storm was loud,

And followed where my banner led ;
He shall my only mourner be,
   And from his pitying eyes shall shed
A soldier's tears for love of me.

O holy Mary, stead me then —
   A simple maid whose heart may fail :
I would not these grim Island men
   Should smile to see my cheek grow pale.
And yet what fairer winding-sheet
   Than martyrs' flame ? What church-yard mould
   More consecrated dust can hold ?
What missal claspeth words more sweet
   To dying ears, than those He spake :
" Blessed are they — yea, doubly blest, —
   Who suffer death for my dear sake.
For them bright crowns and endless rest."

The night is spent. The early gray
   Warms into sunrise in the skies ;
The sunrise of eternal day —
   The threshold steps of paradise.
'Tis written, " After storm comes shine ; "
   Fierce and more fierce the fires may burn,
   But as my limbs to ashes turn,
My soul, O Lord, shall mix with Thine.

Even as yonder trembling star
Melts into morning's golden sea,
 So, rapt through Heavenly spaces far,
Shall this poor life be lost in Thee.

THE LAST OF HIS PEOPLE.

DOWN in the west a kingdom lay,
  Within its coasts tall cities three:
One on a river that flowed from the south,
  One forest-bound on an inland lea,
And one where the southern river's mouth
  Drank the salt flood of the northern sea.
The two were fair as bridesmaids are,
  But how more fair was Kinderlee! —
Their sister bride who glassed her pride
  In the pictured tide of the northern sea.
Through all the years I mourn for thee,
Dear mother-town, lost Kinderlee.

How goodly were her broad church-towers
  And ancient houses ,steeple-high :
Their gable peaks and chimney stacks,
  Where swallows on the wind went by
And storks sat brooding on the thatch
  Were Babels to the burgher's eye :
It seemed, as standing tip-toe there,
  One most could touch the roofing sky.

There sunning on the gargoyled eaves
The doves sat in a patient row,
While Gretchen with the dove-like eyes
Glanced through the lattice down below.

For there in painted garden pots
Sweet smelling herbs and colored blooms
She tended in the window seat;
Such sunshine filled the pleasant rooms.

The shops were fine with webs of price,
And on the market days and fairs
The wooden booths and corner stalls
Held store of town and country wares.

The merchants sent their ventures out
To sail beyond the rounding main:
Out of the south in many days
The ships came faring home again,
Down laden to the water's edge,
With ivory wealth and golden grain.

Secure within the harbor bowl
In hundred holds the freightage lay:
Sweet figs of Smyrna, Muscat gums,
And costly silks from far Cathay.

By noon, by night, thy streets were bright, —
    Gold days and silver eves in thee ;
And music filling day and night
    Made life a song in Kinderlee.

Each hour the holy minster bells
    With soft psalms blessed the upper airs.
The minstrels went about the streets ;
    At noonday in the fountain squares
The maids would set their pitchers down
    To hear the Swedes with yellow hairs,
Or dark Savoyards touch the harp
    And pipe to apes and dancing bears.

When the round moon hung in the lift,
    And lights were out in gay bazaar,
Adown the shadows of the street
    Some northern ballad echoed far
From voices round the threshold stone
    Accordant to the light guitar.

On martyrs' days and holy feasts
    What cheer the simple townsfolk made !
How swelled along the narrow ways
    In civic pomp the plumed parade !

First went the friars six and six,
  With scarlet gowns and shaven polls ;
Above them shone the crucifix
  Where Christ hung bleeding for lost souls.

Next stepped the red-faced trumpeters
  Winding the brazen snaky horn,
And last the mounted men at arms
  With broidered banners high upborne.

On either side, the open doors
  Made frames for happy groups ; down
    rolled
From windows to the street's stone floors,
  Hung rainbow mats and cloths of gold.

Where art thou, O my mother town ?
  The piping winds from off the sea,
That rocked my cradle in thy walls,
  Shall never more blow over thee.
Of all that spoke the kindly speech
  I learned to lisp beside thy knee,
There lives not on the lonely earth
  Or man or wife or child save me.
The tides shift over thy palace stones,
  The grass grows green on Kinderlee.

'T was when the days were waxing long,
  And Lent was now a fortnight old;
When March came in with whistle shrill
And hares were mad and mornings chill;
  The ballads sung and stories told
At Whitsun ales, remembered still,
  And Shrovetide ovens scarce grown cold.

Sudden like wind a trumpet blew:
  The king of all the southern land,
With his stealthy hosts as still as ghosts,
  Crept on to us over the desert sand.

Seven nights had their watch-fires lit the waste,
  Where a thousand tents, like a fleet at sea,
Seemed steering over the barren plain.
  Far off the wolves howled mournfully.

But when the seven days were eight,
  In battle on the red frontier
We met them there, and met swift fate:
  Some fell in fight, some fled in fear.
I saw my king's gray reverend head
  Uplifted on the cruel spear

Discrowned, with bloody hair. Thenceforth
  That grisly standard led the foe,

Its eyes fixed ever on the north,
　As reading all the coming woe.

What boots it tell how Monksbridge fell,
　And Stifton chimneys leaguered long;
How ebbed and flowed the southern tide
　Till, scarce a score of thousands strong,

Before our eyes the wasted land,
　Behind our backs the desert sea,
Grasping a broken, hopeless brand,
　We turned to bay in Kinderlee?

CANTO II.

The Easter evening sun was low,
　The ebb went oozing out the bay,
The shadows of the quiet masts
　Along the quiet water lay.
In that bright evening hush, to stay
Did seem twice sweet, twice hard to go:
　Yet when the wakening Easter day
Shall feel the morning land-breeze blow,
That breeze within our sails shall sing,
　And round our keel shall sing the sea,
And in our wake shall toss and wave
　The beckoning flames of Kinderlee.

Sweet is revenge, the memory sweet
  Of our slain kin; O, sweet to feel
The foeman's stiffening muscles writhe
  In anguish round our smoking steel:

Dear is this little ancient land
  And this old city by the sea;
Yet dearer still our wives, our babes,
  The folk, the tongue of Kinderlee.

Though the brave fear not death, they give
Their lives that those they love may live;
But our lives are too few to save
All that we die for from the grave.

We'll bear our city in our heart
And build it new beyond the sea;
For where we are our land will be, —
There and not here is Kinderlee.

Yet keep once more our Easter eve
  With feast and song; for we will go
With pæans and with joyful hymns
  To Him, who from the Egyptian woe
Exulting led his Israel forth,
  Even from the presence of the foe.

But when the Easter bells give word
  That Christ is risen, and in the east
The dawn hangs its gray signal out;
  Then leave the dance and leave the feast,

And, hastening to the port, embark;
  That ere the morning land breeze die,
Far windward left behind, our home
  May vanish 'twixt the sea and sky.

Only a thin white cloud that crawls
  Into the sky from out the sea,
Will show where smoke the burning walls
  Of our lost city, Kinderlee.

In thee, fair town, we 'll leave behind
  A garrison of faithful fire.
Thou shalt not be the victor's spoil,
  Dear city of our heart's desire.

And now throughout the town each door
  Stood open to the warm spring night,
And festal windows all ablaze
  Made every street an aisle of light.

Across each threshold, where they would,
    The maskers wandered out and in.
Low breathed the passionate soft flute,
    Trembled and wailed the violin.

Yet in the pauses of the dance
    Each ear was listening for a token :
The laugh would turn into a sob,
    The word begun break off unspoken ;
And something in his partner's eye
    Told each the other's heart was broken :

Till, as the night grew deep, a golden
    Curtain rolled across the past.
A strange intoxication came
    And said, " Enjoy !   It is the last."

Sweet riot filled the enfranchised blood
    That in our veins seemed turned to wine ;
The music thrilled exultingly ;
Bacchantic grew the dance and free ;
    The women's eyes began to shine
More brightly through their tears again,
Like moonlight on the falling rain.

Revel so mad, so wild, so sad
  Was never, since the Assyrian king,
While rebels stormed his outer courts,
  Held his last desperate banqueting.

Now I through all the lighted town
  Had joined the maskers here and there;
Had entered many a stranger door,
  And climbed up many an unknown stair.

For all were hosts and guests that night;
  All came and went, without, within;
Welcome to banquet or to dance,
  Alike were comeling, kith and kin.

And many an unacquainted maid,
  Whose beauty to my eyes was new,
Grown sweetly bold and unafraid,
  Gave me the kiss to partners due.

And once I held a rosy pair
  Of palms upon the balcony,
Where silken window curtains sighed
  As the night wind blew off the sea.

I said, " Sweetheart, we meet to part:
  To-morrow on the estranging sea

You will not blush for one more kiss
  You gave me on this balcony."

The lips I kissed were sweet with wine;
  " Here 's no one but the moon, can tell," —
The eyes I kissed were wet with tears;
  She whispered in my arms " Farewell."

But now the lamps burned large and dim;
  Muffled in yellow mist they shone;
The dancers seemed to wave and swim;
  Their voices took a drowsy tone.

The music sounded from far off
  Like music that one hears in dreams.
Narcotic grew the ball-room flowers;
  The lustres shed unearthly gleams.

Heavy mine eyelids grew with sleep,
  My heart forgot both joy and pain, —
To-night, to-morrow, yesterday, —
  As though an opiate touched my brain.

I wandered from the crowded rooms,
  And groped through darkened corridors,
And stumbled up long staircases,
  Until I reached the upper floors;

And found a chamber far apart,
  Where neither light nor sound there came;
And fell upon the bed and sunk
  To sleep, as sinks a dying flame.

CANTO III.

In weary dreams I seemed to hear
  The ring of bells and trumpets blown,
And voices calling, and the tramp
  Of feet upon the pavement stone.

And then I fathomed darker gulfs
  Of sleep, too deep for dreams to sound;
Until mine eyes unclosed and traced
  The figures on the carpet's ground,

And idly watched a shadow vine,
  Whose leaves did tremble evermore
Within the square of still sunshine
  That lay upon the chamber floor.

But suddenly I started up;
  My heart stopped — like a deadly pain
That anodynes have put to sleep,
  My thoughts came piercing back again.

I tottered to the window seat:
    The port was empty, and the town
As silent in the broad full light
    As though the midnight stars shone down.

Far off a hundred sunlit sails
    Before the wind were running free,
Like flocks that browsing westward go
    On the blue pasture of the sea.

As when a mother stands beside
    Her darling's open grave, and hears
The priest speak words of holy cheer;
    Then softly come her sobs and tears:—

But when into the grave they lower
    The little body of her child,
She thinks, "O never, never more, —
    My baby!" and her grief grows wild:

Even so my great despair was dumb,
    Until behind the rounding sea
The last sail vanished, with its freight
    Of all that made life dear to me.

And then my agony broke forth
    In groans and cries and hopeless prayers;

But suddenly I started up
  And hurried down the winding stairs,

And through the halls, where still the lamps
  Burned sickly in the white sunshine,
And flowers lay fading on the board,
  With cups half emptied of their wine.

I ran down all the silent streets,
  And through the echoing market-place :
No shopman in his doorway lounged,
  No window held the gossip's face.

The dead walls answered back my shouts :
  Where the tall houses leaned together
Floated across the strip of sky
  A white smoke, curling like a feather.

In every house the door stood wide,
  The clocks were ticking on the wall,
The playthings strewed the nursery floor, —
  Here lay a hat and there a shawl.

It seemed as though the inmates had
  But stepped into the other room ; —
Shall I not find the goodwife there,
  Or busy housemaid with her broom?

Each home was with some presence warm
   Whose life was here but yesterday;
Whose very pressure, mould and form
   Still fresh on bed or sofa lay,
Whose image from the mirror's face
   Seemed hardly to have passed away.

But now, as heavier plumes of smoke
   Across the windows drifting came,
I mounted to the housetop high,
   And saw where lines of sieging flame

Which all along the landward wall
   Our men had kindled through the town,
With ever widening wings of smoke
   Spread to the wind, sailed slowly down.

At moments when a fiercer gust
   The sooty curtain blew aside,
On the plain's utmost southern edge
   In the strong sunlight I descried

Something like steel that glittered, where
   The vanguard of the foe came on.
Too late! The ocean and the air
   Had snatched the prize his arms had won.

THE LAST OF HIS PEOPLE.

At evening from the neighboring hill
I marked their watch-fires circling far.
The rising tide, the river's flow
Came upward from the dark below;
  Over the ruins smouldering still
Hung in the west the evening star, —
  A burning candle in the hand
  Of a vast form that seemed to stand
Treading the sunset's hem,
  Ready to light me on to them
Who in the black deep wandering are.

O planet, let me follow; take
Me with thee in thy shining wake!
Thou settest here, but risest there
Amid the ocean's twilight, where
Upon the deck dim figures stand,
  Whisper and weep and talk of me.
"Whether has he been left on land,
  Or is he somewhere on the sea
Among the vessels of the fleet?"
"Trust me, he is; and we shall meet
  In port at last, if not before.
So dry your tears, it will be sweet,
Dear mother, sister, friends, to greet
  Our lost one at the port once more."

Alas! no tongue of man can tell
  What port that far-bound navy made.
  No whaler, slaver, bark of trade,
Cruising for strange outlandish freight
In each remotest sound and strait
  And archipelago, hath spoken
A single sail from Kinderlee.
  The land's last corner gives no token,
Nor the uncommunicable sea.

These many years I haunt the wharves
  And marts of every seaport town,
And question sailors in the street
For news of that long-vanished fleet, —
  The Portuguese, tattooed and brown,
Seal-fishers, Holland skippers old,
With queues and earrings of rough gold,
Whose keels are thick with shells and weed
  From Indian harbors, — all in vain:
  On northern fiord or tropic main
  No lookout yet hath seen them run
  Close hauled or free, by moon or sun,
  Windward or leeward e'er again.

Yet hope will tell how still they dwell
  Within a loftier Kinderlee,

On some green isle or some rich shore,
  Unknown, beyond the western sea.

And when glad death shall close mine eyes,
  O Christ, though bright thy kingdom be,
Yet ope them not in Paradise
  But in that other Kinderlee.

COLLEGE RIMES.

THE DARKE LADYE.

A shadow haunts about my door,
  In midnight dreams I see
An Afrite-woman pace the floor : —
  It is the Darke Ladye !

Of mournful sable is her robe :
  Her eyes like waves are rolled
Full whitely ; from her ear's black lobe
  Hangs down the red, red gold.

The clothe-baskét is in her hand,
  The tear is in her e'e :
Her children two behind her stand
  While speaks the Darke Ladye :

" Full thrice with round, vermilion face
  Behind the cedars black,
The moon hath risen in her place
  On broad Quinnipiac.

" Full fourscore dawns have streaked the bay
  Since thou, upon thy knee,

Didst vow the red, red gold to pay
Unto the Darke Ladye.

"I washed from soil and inky blots,
   Thy cuffs and eke thy shirt;
The Æthiop changed another's spots
   And cleansed the stranger's dirt.

"And though thy stains as scarlet were,
   With blood of strawberry,
All snowy grew each handkercher
   Before the Darke Ladye.

"But now, my hearth is desolate
   And on the Elm Street shore,
The brooms are still; my dusky mate
   Shall beat the rug no more.

"Look on these cherubs, short but sweet;
   How hangs each curly head!
Their eyes are dim with tears; they eat
   The orphan's gingerbread.

"The while thou smok'st the costly weed,
   (I see one on thy shelf)
Thou makest widows' hearts to bleed
   Withholding of thy pelf.

"False caitiff! didst thou not declare
    A check was on the way
From thy far boyhood's home, and swear
    To pay me yesterday?

"Henceforth no soap thy sheets shall know,
    No starch thy limp wrist-band,
And dirty towels in a row
    Shall hang on thy wash-stand."

She's gone, the door behind her slams;
    Her feet descend the stair,
And I with sulphurous loud damns
    Disturb the upper air.

She comes at morn and dewy eve,
    She comes just after tea,
To stand beside my door and grieve,
    That dismal Darke Ladye.

Thrice have I sent her small, small bill
    For my dear Pa to see.
Some happy chance bring back his check
    To quit the Darke Ladye.

YE LAYE OF YE WOODPECKORE.

O WHITHER goest thou, pale studént
    Within the wood so fur?
Art on the chokesome cherry bent?
    Dost seek the chestnut burr?

PALE STUDENT.

O it is not for the mellow chestnút
    That I so far am come,
Nor yet for puckery cherries, but
    For Cypripediúm.

A blossom hangs the choke-cherry
    And eke the chestnut burr,
And thou a silly fowl must be,
    Thou red-head wood-peckér.

PICUS ERYTHROCEPHALUS.

Turn back, turn back, thou pale studént,
    Nor in the forest go;
There lurks beneath his bosky tent
    The deadly mosquitó,

And there the wooden-chuck doth tread,
    And from the oak-tree's top
The red, red squirrels on thy head
    The frequent acorn drop.

PALE STUDENT.

The wooden-chuck is next of kin
    Unto the wood-peckér: .
I fear not thine ill-boding din,
    And why should I fear her?

What though a score of acorns drop
    And squirrels' fur be red!
'Tis not so ruddy as thy top —
    So scarlet as thy head.

O rarely blooms the Cypripe-
    diúm upon its stalk;
And like a torch it shines to me
    Adown the dark wood-walk.

O joy to pluck it from the ground,
    To view the purple sac,
To touch the sessile stigma's round —
    And shall I then turn back?

PICUS ERYTHROCEPHALUS.

O black and shining is the bog
   That feeds the sumptuous weed,
Nor stone is found nor bedded log
   Where foot may well proceed.

Midmost it glimmers in the mire
   Like Jack o' Lanthorn's spark,
Lighting with phosphorescent fire
   The green umbrageous dark.

There while thy thirsty glances drink
   The fair and baneful plant,
Thy shoon within the ooze shall sink
   And eke thine either pant.

PALE STUDENT.

Give o'er, give o'er, thou wood-peckóre;
   The bark upon the tree
Thou, at thy will, mayst peck and bore,
   But peck and bore not me.

Full two long hours I 've searched about
   And 'twould in sooth be rum,
If I should now go back without
   The Cypripedíum.

PICUS ERYTHROCEPHALUS.

Farewell! Farewell! But this I tell
  To thee, thou pale studént,
Ere dews have fell, thou'lt rue it well
  That woodward thou didst went:

Then whilst thou blows the drooping nose
  And wip'st the pensive eye —
There where the sad *Symplocarpus fœtidus*
    grows,
  Then think — O think of I!

Loud flouted there that student wight
  Swich warnynge for to hear;
"I scorn, old hen, thy threats of might,
  And eke thine ill grammére.

"Go peck the lice (or green or red)
  That swarm the bass-wood tree,
But wag no more thine addled head
  Nor clack thy tongue at me."

The wood-peck turned to whet her beak,
  The student heard her drum,
As through the wood he went to seek
  The Cypripediúm.

Alas! and for that pale studént:
　The evening bell did ring,
And down the walk the Freshmen went
　Unto the prayer-meetíng;

Upon the fence loud rose the song,
　The weak, weak tea was o'er —
Ha! who is he that sneaks along
　Into South Middle's door?

The mud was on his shoon, and O!　·
　The briar was in his thumb,
His staff was in his hand, but no —
　No Cypripediúm.

A MERRY BALLAD OF THREE SOPHO-
MORES AND A TOLL-WOMAN.

IT is a lordly sophomore,
  The thirstiest one of three,
And he hath.stopped at the toll-house door
  All under the greenwood tree.

"Come hither, come hither, my merrymen both
  And stand on either side:
What see ye on the toll-house wall
  By the toll-house door so wide?"

They ha' lookit north — they ha' lookit south —
  They ha' lookit aboon the sky:
Then up and spake the first merryman
  And thus he made reply: —

"I ha' lookit north — I ha' lookit south —
  I ha' lookit aboon the sky,
Yet I see naught on the toll-house wall
  Or the toll-house door thereby."

Then up and spake the next merryman
With " Alack and woe betide !
For I've left my glass on the green, green grass
All by the burnie's side.

" So though I look north and though I look south,
And though I look straight before,
I see nothing at all on the toll-house wall
Nor yet on the toll-house door."

" Now shame ! now shame ! my merrymen both,
For see ye not written here
These words that tell of cakes to sell,
And eke of the small, small beer ?

" ' I have never a penny left in my purse —
Never a penny but three,
And one is brass and another is lead,
And another is white monéy.'

" But haud out your pouches o' gude green silk,
Or the skin of the red deer fleet,
And we'se tak' a draught of the wee sma' beer
And a bite of the seed-cake sweet."

He hadna rapped a rap, a rap, —
A rap but only three,

When out and came the toll-house dame,
  Was a grisly wight to see.

Her cheek was yellow, her throat was lean,
  Her eyes "baith blear and blin':"
No Soph hath half the beard, I ween,
  That flourished on her chin.

"A boon ! A boon ! thou toll-woman,
  A boon thou'se give to me,
For a thirstier soul than I am one
  • Lives not in Christianté.

"I 've swallowed the sassafras in the wood
  And the dust on the king's highway,
And the sorrel that grows on the sandy bank,
  Till my throat is as dry as hay."

"O seek ye of the red, red wine,
  Or seek ye of the white,
To moisten your dainty clay withal,
  And your whistles both shrill and slight?"

"We seek not of the red, red wine —
  We seek not of the white :

We seek but a draught of the small, small beer,
Of the seed-cake only a bite."

"Then show me the red, red gold," quo' she,
" And show me the silver fine,
And show me a roll of the green, green back,
Or you 'se get no beer of mine."

Then up and spake the first merryman, —
By several saints he swore ; —
" I have but an Index-check [1] in my pouch,
And the devil a penny more."

Then up and spake the next merryman —
" And I 've but a soda-ticket,
And a crumpled two-cent revenue stamp
With no gum-stickum to stick it."

" Aroint ! — Aroint ! ye beggarly loons,
From under my threshold tree !
What good to me is a revenue stamp
Or an Index-check perdy?

[1] Entitling the holder to one *Index to the Yale Literary Magazine*, prepared by "the busy L. H. B." These checks were thrown on the market in great numbers, and rapidly depreciated, causing a panic in the class only equalled by the similar distress produced by the famous " Finley Issue " in the class of '66.

"A soda ticket? A soda fiddle-
　　Stick! Pesky belly-wash!
Them folks as like it may swill sich fizz,
　　In their stomachs to rumble and swash :

"But as for me, I 'll stick to my cider,
　　And eke to the small, small beer,
And sell it to them as have money to pay;
　　But you — get out o' here!"

Then beerless to the dusty road
　　Turned each bold Sophomore,
While with a slam behind him closed
　　The heavy toll-house door.

A FISH STORY.

A WHALE of great porosity
  And small specific gravity,
Dived down with much velocity
  Beneath the sea's concavity.

But soon the weight of water
  Squeezed in his fat immensity,
Which varied — as it ought to—
  Inversely as his density.

It would have moved to pity
  An Ogre or a Hessian,
To see poor Spermaceti
  Thus suffering compression.

The while he lay a-roaring
  In agonies gigantic,
The lamp-oil out came pouring
  And greased the wide Atlantic.

(Would we 'd been in the Navy,
  And cruising there! Imagine us
All in a sea of gravy,
  With billow oleaginous!)

At length old million-pounder,
  Low on a bed of coral,
Gave his last dying flounder,
  Whereto I pen this moral.

MORAL.

O let this tale dramatic
  Anent this whale Norwegian,
And pressures hydrostatic
  Warn you, my young collegian,

That down-compelling forces
  Increase as you get deeper;
The lower down your course is,
  The upward path 's the steeper.

LOST LETTERS OF THE GREEK ALPHABET.

Dim is my damp eye
For thee, O Sampi:
Lo! here I drop a
Tear for Koppa;
Gone, too, art thou,
Departed Vau;
(Ah! letter sweet,
Now obsolete.)
Ye-one-two-three
All vanished be,
Swallowed by Time's much-gulping sea.

F,

But thou, Digamma —
Chiefly for thee
We wail and clamour
In threnody.
Old Hell, thy gammer,
Swallowed thee whole;

Yet still thy soul
Doth haunt this grammar —
A ghostly V
For whom Prof. Hadley
Moaneth madly
And in each dark hiatus sadly
Listens for thee.
Ever for thee.

A HOLIDAY ECLOGUE.

First Mason:

Tink-a-link! Tink-a-link! Hear the trowels ring;
Feel the merry breezes make the scaffold swing;
See the skimming swallow brush us with her
    wing : —
Go it with your hammers, boys; time us while
    we sing.

BELOW.
First Student:

See the yellow sparkle of the Neckar in the
    glass,
    And through the cedar branches sparkles blue
      the sea;
Hear the sweet piano — hear the German lass
    Sing *Freut' euch des Lebens* — Oh ! " I love, 1
      love the free ! "

Second Student:

    I like the canary better;
      Look, how he swells his throttle !
    He gurgles like musical water
      That dances and sings in a bottle.

ABOVE.

Second Mason:

D'ye mind the students down in the grove
Drinking their wine and beer?
That's an easy life they lead.

First Mason:

So do we up here
When the weathercock points west
And the look-off's clear.

Third Mason:

House-top Jim's the boy for work!

First Mason:

True for you, my dear.
(*Whistles " The Girl I Left Behind me."*)

BELOW.

First Student:

See the Dutchmen on those settees:
Is n't it like the Rhine?
And the old church-tower up over the trees —
Kellner ! Noch ein Stein !

Third Student:

I'd like to work with those masons there
Half way up the sky.
The air is sweet where the pigeons build,
And the world is all in their eye.

Second Student:

But " Love is of the valley:" the Gretchen and
    the Kellner
Haunt the cheerful levels of the lower story.
Glory in the garret — comfort in the cellar:
I will keep the comfort — you may take the
    glory.

ABOVE.

First Mason:

Look up at the pointers: they 're drawing close
    together;
'T is here we get the earliest news of sun, and
    moon, and weather;
We can hear time's pulse a-ticking, with the
    whistling weathercock.
Drop your mortar-boards, my lads, it's coming
    twelve o'clock.

Third Mason:

Oh! it 's hungry that I am with working in the
    wind,
But there 's a shawl and bonnet — below there:
    do you mind?
It 's Molly with the dinner-pail: she 's coming in
    the door.
Faith, my belly thinks my throat is cut this half
    an hour and more.

(*The church clock strikes the noon.*)

AD IULUM ANTONIUM.

HORACE'S ODES : LIBER IV.   CARMEN II.

Tony, for me to write an ode,
   And spout it from a staging
Would be to trust in waxen wings,[1]
   Or, when the winds are raging,
To pull outside the Light-house Point
   In Charlie's paper wherry
(Six inches and a half across ;)
   'T would be imprudent — very !

"Weak-winged is song ; " Why don't you get
   Some muse with pinions tougher ? —
Some epic dominie or some
   Didactic-blank-verse buffer,
Complacent, fat, in white cravat,
   Who, in mid-climax soaring,
Will pause to hear his audience cheer
   And kick upon the flooring.

[1] " Ceratis ope Dædalea
Nititur pennis."

Get some prize-poet who can write
   A dozen different metres.
There's Finch; there's Duffield — Hollister
   Who does our best Phi Betas;
There's Edward Sill — he slings a quill
   Quite filthy (perhaps *stylus*
Would sound more classical than quill;)
   There's Rev. Crescentius Nilus;—

That swelling Nile [1] whose annual flood
   The "Courant" always mentions,
Enriching drear alumni feeds
   And Delta Phi conventions.
I name a laureate here and there;
   You'll doubtless think of others.
Who did the anniversary
   (No joke on *verse*) at Brothers?

These swans [2] of song I often see
   Early some autumn morning
Fly over in the frosty sky;
   Faint sounds their leader's warning.

---

[1] " Monte decurrens velut amnis, imbres
      Quem super notas aluere ripas."
[2] "Multa Dircæum levat aura cycnum."

Southward they seek the Chesapeake,
  To winter homes returning,
Above the maple-forests red
  And brushwood swamps a-burning.

But I, a bee[1] that shuns the wind,
  By East Rock's sheltered bases
Crawl into spurs of columbines
  In warm and sunny places,
Humming in slender, earthy strain
  Of little cells I 'm building
At home, and how my jacket brown
  Has one small stripe of gilding.

Perchance on some Red Letter night
  When snow was softly heaping
Outside upon the window-sill,
  And, o'er our senses creeping,
The sleepy malt, the grate-fire's glow
  That tinged our pipe smoke rosy
As evening clouds, had made us feel
  Particularly cosy,

I 've taken from my pocket's depths
  A torn and crumpled paper

[1] " Ego apis Matinæ," etc

Whereon were traced some idle rhymes,
  An idler brain's light vapor;
And if to these the Letters Red
  Listened with kind indulgence,[1]
We'll lay it to that genial malt
  And fire-light's soft effulgence.

But when in gilt-edged album-book
  I'm asked to write a sonnet,
I sadly shake my head and say
  "Dear Miss, I am not on it."
And when Dick reads me his new pome
  In twenty cantos, then ah!
My little chirping muse descries
  · How *tenuis* is her *penna.*

[1] " Si quid loquar audiendum," etc

HIGH ISLAND.

PLEASANT it was at shut of day,
When wind and wave had sunk away,
To hear, as on the rocks we lay,
    The fog bell toll;
And grimly through the gathering night
The horn's dull blare from Faulkner's Light,
Snuffed out by ghostly fingers white
    That round it stole.

Somewhere behind its curtain, soon
The mist grew conscious of a moon:
No more we heard the diving loon
    Scream from the spray;
But seated round our drift-wood fire
Watched the red sparks rise high and higher,
Then, wandering into night, expire
    And pass away.

Down the dark wood, the pines among,
A lurid glare the firelight flung;
So for a while we talked and sung,
    And then to sleep;

And heard in dreams the light-house bell,
As all night long in solemn swell
The tidal waters rose and fell
    With soundings deep.

LOTUS EATING.

COME up once more before mine eyes,
  Sweet halcyon days, warm summer sea,
Faint orange of the morning skies
  And dark-lined shores upon the lee!
Touched with the sunrise, sea and sky
All still on Memory's canvas lie:
The scattered isles with India ink
Dot the wide back-ground's gold and pink:
Unstirring in the Sunday calm,
  Their profile cedars, sharply drawn,
  Bold black against the flushing dawn,
Take shape like clumps of tropic palm.
Night shadows still the distance dim
(Ultra-marine) where ocean's brim
Upholdeth the horizon-rim.

Once more in thought we seem to creep
  By lonely reefs where sea-birds scream,
Ulysses-like, along the deep
  Borne onward in the ocean-stream.

The sea-floor spreadeth glassy still ;
No breath the idle sail doth fill ;
Our oar-blades smite the heavy seas ;
Under the world the morning breeze
Treads with the sun the unknown ways.
  Thus steer we o'er the solemn main
  Eating the Lotus-fruit again,
Dreaming that time forever stays,
Singing "Where, Absence, is thy sting!"
Listening to hear our echoes ring
Through the far rocks where Sirens sing.

THE MERMAID'S GLASS.

'T was down among the Thimble Isles,
That strew for many " liquid miles "
The waters of Long Island Sound :
Our yacht lay in a cove ; around
The rocky isles with cedars green
And channels winding in between :
And here a low, black reef was spread,
And there a sunken " nigger-head "
Dimpled the surface of the tide.
From one tall island's cliffy side
We heard the shaggy goats that fed :
The gulls wheeled screaming overhead
Or settled in a snowy flock
Far out upon the lonely rock
Which, like a pillar, seemed to show
Some drowned acropolis below.
Meanwhile, in the warm sea about,
With many a plunge and jolly shout,
Our crew enjoyed their morning bath.
The hairy skipper in his wrath

Lay cursing on the gunwale's rim :
He loved a dip but could not swim ;
So, now and then with plank afloat
He 'd struggle feebly round the boat
And o'er the side climb puffing in,
Scraping wide areas off his skin,
Then lie and sun each hirsute limb
Once more upon the gunwale's rim
And shout, with curses unavailing,
" Come out ! There 's wind : let 's do some sail-
    ing."
A palm-leaf hat, that here and there
Bobbed on the water, showed him where
Some venturous swimmer outward bound
Escaped beyond his voice's sound.
All heedless of their skipper's call,
One group fought for the upset yawl.
The conqueror sat astride the keel
And deftly pounded with his heel
The hands that clutched his citadel,
Which showed — at distance — like the shell
Round which, unseen, the Naiad train
Sport naked on the middle main.
Myself had drifted far away,
Meanwhile, from where the sail-boat lay,
Till all unbroken I could hear
The wave's low whisper in my ear,

And at the level of mine eye
The blue vibration met the sky.
Sometimes upon my back I lay
And watched the clouds, while I and they
Were wafted effortless along. —
Sudden I seemed to hear a song:
Yet not a song, but some weird strain
As though the inarticulate main
Had found a voice whose human tone
Interpreted its own dull moan;
Its foamy hiss; its surfy roar;
Its gentle lapping on the shore;
Its noise of subterranean waves
That grumble in the sea-cliff caves;
Its whish among the drifting miles
Of gulf-wind from the Indian Isles: —
All — all the harmonies were there
Which ocean makes with earth or air.
Turning I saw a sunken ledge
Bared by the ebb, along whose edge
The matted sea-weed dripped: thereon,
Betwixt the dazzle of the sun
And the blue shimmer of the sea,
I saw — or else I seemed to see
A mermaid, crooning a wild song,
Combing with arm uplifted long

The hair that shed its meshes black
Down the slope whiteness of her back.
She held a mirror in her hand,
Wherein she viewed sky, sea, and land,
Her beauty's background and its frame.
But now, as toward the rock I came,
All 'suddenly across the glass
Some startling image seemed to pass;
For her song rose into a scream,
Over her shoulders one swift gleam
Of eyes unearthly fell on me,
And, 'twixt the flashing of the sea
And the blind dazzle of the sun,
I saw the rock, but thereupon
She sat no longer 'gainst the blue ;
Only across the reef there flew
One snow-white tern and vanished too.
But, coasting that lone island round,
Among the slippery kelp I found
A little oval glass that lay
Upturned and flashing in the ray
Of the down-looking sun. Thereto
With scarce believing eyes I drew
And took it captive.

A while there
I rested in the mermaid's lair,

And felt the merry breeze that blew,
And watched the sharpies as they flew,
And snuffed the sea's breath thick with brine,
And basked me in the sun's warm shine;
Then with my prize I made my way
Once more to where the sail-boat lay.
I kept the secret — and the glass;
By day across its surface pass
The transient shapes of common things
Which chance within its oval brings.
But when at night I strive to sound
The darkness of its face profound,
Again I seem to hear the breeze
That curls the waves on summer seas;
I see the isles with cedars green;
The channels winding in between;
The coves with beaches of white sand;
The reefs where warning spindles stand;
And, through the multitudinous shimmer
Of waves and sun, again the glimmer
Of eyes unearthly falls on me,
Deep with the mystery of the sea.

A MEMORY.

I came across the marsh to-night,
   And though the wind was cold,
I stayed a moment on the bridge
   To note the paly gold

That lingered on the darkening bay;
   The creek which ran below
Was frozen dumb; the dreary flats
   Were overspread with snow.

The college bell began to ring,
   And as the north wind blew
Its distant janglings out to sea,
   I thought, dear Friend, of you;

And how one warm September day,
   While yet the woods were green,
We strayed across the happy hills
   And this wide marsh between.

The hay-stacks dotted here and there
　The water-meadows wide :
The even lines of sluices black
　Were filling with the tide.

Then this salt stream, now winter-bound,
　Fled softly through the sedge,
Retreating from the sparkling Sound ;
　And there along its edge

We strolled, and marked the far-off sloops,
　And watched the cattle graze.
O'erhead the swallows rushed in troops,
　While bright with purple haze,

West Rock looked down the winding plain —
　Ah ! this was long ago ;
The summer's gone, and you are gone,
　As everything must go.

PRESENTATION DAY, 1868.

Their songs are done, their forms are gone,
   And Time for us hath turned the glass:
We heed not, as we take their seats,
   How downward swift the red sands pass.

We heed not how the cloud comes on
   That shadows all the sunny land—
The day when heart from heart must part
   And clinging hand unlink from hand.

What shall that Dies Iræ give
   In place of that it takes away:
How fill the time we have to live
   While youth treads downward to decay?

Good-by, true friend; Good-by, old Yale;
   Good-by, each dear familiar spot;
Good-by, sweet season of our youth—
   "The golden, happy, unforgot."

IVY ODE.

CLASS DAY, 1869.

WHEN we are gone from sight and mind,
Leaving no token here behind
To speak for us in this loved scene,
O, Ivy, keep our memory green;
And trace in thy soft, leafy line,
The dear old name of Sixty-nine.

When youth and Yale are far away,
And these young heads are growing gray,
We'll think, how on this cold stone wall
Our Ivy climbeth strong and tall;
And then our hearts, like thee, shall grow
The greener for the winter snow.

Farewell! Farewell! A leaf from thee
In after years a charm shall be
To start the tear in eyes long dry;
To stir the drowsy memory
With sad, sweet thoughts of Auld Lang Syne,
And friends we loved in Sixty-nine.

THE NEW YALE.

ALL day we hear the chisels ring,
The windlass creak, the masons sing;
With every brightening moon there falls
A longer shadow from the walls.
We hope these rising halls may bring
Some new event — some wished-for thing.
We look to see that not alone
Of mellow brick-work or of stone,
But reared by wisdom's magic wands
Invisible, not made with hands,
Yet stronger than the trowel builds,
Deep-laid by toiling scholar-guilds,
Her corner-stone's free-masonry
As broad as this brave century,
Our new, regenerate Yale shall be —
Our Yankee university.
O let her widened portals stand
All opening on the future's land;
Her pointed windows one by one
Steal color from the setting sun;

Her gables and her belfries high,
Her generous chimney-stacks whereby
The college doves shall build and fly,
Front only toward the western sky;
And far above her tall elm trees
The bright vanes point the western breeze!
We care not that the dawn should throw
Its gilding on our portico;
But rather that our natal star,
Bright Hesper, in the twilight far
Should beckon toward the imperial West
Which he, our Berkeley, loved the best;
Whereto, his mighty line doth say,
" The course of empire takes its way."
For in the groves of that young land
A lordly school his wisdom planned
To teach new knowledge to new men,
Fresh sciences undreamed of then.
She comes — had come unknown before,
Though not on " vext Bermoothe's " shore.
Yet will she not her prophet fail —
The new — the old — the same dear Yale.

www.ingramcontent.com/pod-product-compliance
Lightning Source LLC
Chambersburg PA
CBHW030610270326
41927CB00007B/1117